the
essence
of
style

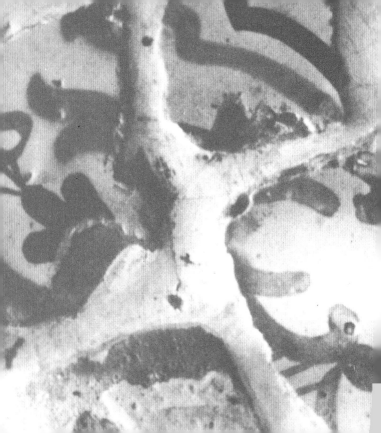

the essence of
ITALIAN
COUNTRY

CATHERINE SABINO AND GUY BOUCHET

THAMES AND HUDSON

First published in Great Britain in 1995 by Thames and Hudson Ltd, London by arrangement with Clarkson N. Potter, Inc./Publishers, 201 East 50th Street, New York, NY 10022.

British Library Cataloguing-in-Publication Data

A catalogue record for this book is available from the British Library.

ISBN 0-500-27855-5

Printed and bound in China

CONTENTS

INTRODUCTION

Italians have turned their passion for living into an art, and nowhere is their instinctive skill for la dolce vita *so pure and exuberant as it is in the countryside.* Italian Country *celebrates the extraordinary appeal and variety of the Italian countryside through its people, houses, decorations, crafts, and cuisine.*

Country style in Italy—more than in France, England, or the United States—varies from region to region. Italians have come late to a country style that celebrates a rural past, but the recent passion for restored farmhouses furnished with rustic pieces signals a new taste for a less sophisticated way of life. A bucolic style also prevails in mountain resorts, although the look is dressed up considerably more than in Tuscany or Umbria.

The formality and graciousness of the northern lake regions is embodied in their stately, classically proportioned lakeside villas, delicate antique furnishings, and formal gardens. It is a lavish area, built by an Italian—or more pre-

*cisely, European—elite. One Milanese described an impos-
ing villa he inherited from his grandfather and justified the
taste for grandeur it reveals: "They wanted the same stan-
dard of gracious living they enjoyed in town houses and the
city palazzi. They didn't want to experience any 'entry'
shock when coming to the country for vacations."*

*Most 19th-century seaside dwellings along the Riviera or
the Amalfi coast are less grand than villas on the lakes, but
an Old World ambiance lingers in certain Mediterranean
resort houses. Palazzi bordering the harbors and shores of
the Italian peninsula were built in the last two hundred
years, villas high in the mountains were built after World
War II, and those along Sardinia's Costa Smeralda and
Porto Rotono orginated in the 1960s. In desirable spots like
Portofino and Positano, new construction and the alteration
of existing structures are now prohibited by local preserva-
tion groups.*

*Prior to World War II only a handful of Italians could
afford a villa in the countryside. Postwar prosperity and
land reformation acts allowed thousands to buy and restore*

houses in rural areas or by the sea. Starting in the 1950s, the casa colonica, *or farmhouse, was no longer the exclusive domain of the farmer. With the* mezzadria *(sharecropping system) abolished, 60,000 farmhouses came onto the market in Tuscany and Umbria when farmers moved to towns in search of salaried work. A handful of medieval towers, and even small castles, have also been available for purchase in the Italian countryside, and despite their more august pasts, these buildings are often in a state of greater disrepair than the average* casa colonica. *But while the tower, castle, and abbey can be made into interesting and often imposing homes, it is the restored farmhouse that is the archetypal country residence in the central Italian countryside.*

Visiting a range of houses in Tuscany and Umbria, in the lake region, in the mountains, and by the sea, Italian Country *invites readers to bring the warmth, spirit, and color of the Italian countryside into their own homes.*

PRECEDING PAGES: *One wing of the Villa d'Este hotel on Lake Como has a trompe l'oeil façade and Gothic and Renaissance details.*

LOOKING OUTSIDE

To the first-time traveler, Italy's treasures may seem to lie in her spendid cities, in her churches filled with mosaics and frescoes, and in her museums and galleries. But for many people who have come to know the peninsula better, her most abundant riches lie in her varied countryside.

Consider Tuscany's and Umbria's gentle landscapes, where feathery cypresses, shimmery olive trees, and vineyards cover rolling sepia-toned hills; or the mountains, the jagged and silver southern Alps and the rosy Dolomite massifs, dotted with villages steeped in folklore and tradition. Then there is the Italian lake region, a seductive geographical blend of northern and southern Europe, where pine trees and Alpine vistas form a backdrop for palm tree–lined quays, stately villas, and semitropical gardens. And there are such famous Mediterranean regions as the Riviera, the Amalfi coast, and the island of Sardinia, with their jewel-toned waters, pastel-tinted villages, and harrowing cliff-hugging roads with glorious views. The Italian writer Giovanni Papini noted that his homeland had "woody vales like Scandinavia, heaths as in Scotland, orange-scented woods as in Andalusia, serene hills covered with olive groves and vineyards like Greece [and] flowering woods like Japan," among countless other delights.

The Italian countryside can easily be enjoyed whether one has a little or a lot of time. One can delight in an afternoon drive through Chianti country in Tuscany, visit a medieval hill town in Umbria, relax for a weekend in a grand Old World–style hotel overlooking a magnificent lake, spend the month of August exploring the rugged and fashionable aspects of Sardinia, or head to the Alps for a weekend of skiing. For the artist the Italian countryside can often serve as a muse.

This bounty of natural beauty makes Italy an irresistible lure for people from around the world. Even sophisticated and well-traveled Italians feel that the most enchanting earthly treasures lie right at home.

PRECEDING PAGES: *A view of Positano from a hillside villa.*

VIEWS

ABOVE: *The sheltered harbor of Portofino, in northern Italy, attracts a mix of international yachts, which are moored next to local fishing boats.* **RIGHT:** *Throughout the Italian countryside, the roofs of houses are covered with rounded terra-cotta tiles.* **PRECEDING PAGES:** *In the Chianti district of Tuscany, feathery cypresses surround a large stone* fattoria, *or farmhouse.*

ABOVE: *An arched window in the bell tower of the Badia a Coltibuono chapel in Tuscany frames the Chianti landscape.* **RIGHT:** *The roof of the Mantegazza villa on Lake Como. The terra-cotta tiles provide good insulation, and their rounded shape allows rainwater to drain off easily.*

Life on the Mediterranean and lake coastlines is both sophisticated and simple. **CLOCKWISE FROM TOP LEFT:** *Cabanas line the shore near Portofino; a terrace of Villa d'Este provides a view across Lake Como; small and large boats are at home along the Riviera.* **FAR LEFT:** *Fishing villages like Portofino have become famous resorts.*

ABOVE: *An antique bell stands out against the stark white stone and stucco roof of a house in Praiano, a village along the Amalfi Drive.*
RIGHT: *The rooftop of the same villa, the Frigeri house. Like many villas along the Amalfi coast, it was built on a rocky cliff that descends toward the sea.*

Above: *The Borromeo Palace dominates the tiny island of Isola Bella in the middle of Lake Maggiore.* **Left:** *The medieval town of Orvieto, perched on a wide base of volcanic rock, is one of Umbria's most impressive sites. The 14th-century Gothic cathedral has a brilliant façade adorned with multicolored mosaics and marbles.*

25

During the week, the waters of Lake Como are tranquil. On weekends, the lake is crisscrossed by pleasure craft, hydrofoils, and ferries, which stop at towns along the shore.

Above: *The little ochre-toned Church of St. George in Portofino.* **Right:** *Because of the lack of flat terrain surrounding Lake Como, villages and churches hug the shore and many houses are built on steep hills and mountain slopes.*

ABOVE: *Reminders of a medieval past in an Umbrian hill town: densely packed, narrow stone houses.* **RIGHT:** *Terra-cotta roof tiles, weathered over the centuries.*

30

LEFT: *A detail of a fanciful wrought-iron gate in Courmayeur.* **BELOW:** *The outdoor dining area of a restaurant in Portofino.*

ABOVE: *Snow-topped cloisters and a chapel abut the Tondani villa in Poussey, a residential district of Courmayeur.* **LEFT:** *The heart of Cortina d'Ampezzo has retained its Alpine flavor despite the resort's international fame and considerable development.*

CLOCKWISE FROM TOP LEFT: *A narrow street in Courmayeur; the Italian Alps, which include some of the highest peaks in Europe; a village church near Cortina d'Ampezzo.* **FAR RIGHT:** *A small sled lies abandoned near the woods surrounding the chalet owned by the Marzotto family in Cortina d'Ampezzo.*

The people who live in the Italian countryside contribute to its warmth. **CLOCKWISE FROM TOP LEFT:** Fioretta Panerai, at her Tuscan farmhouse; a farmer's son; Nanni Gori, a Castellare farmer. **FAR LEFT, CLOCKWISE FROM TOP LEFT:** A sailor in Portofino; a Ligurian fisherman; Giacomo Mantegazza, heading to his Lake Como villa; an artisan at work.

37

During the week of the vendemmia, *farmhands spend long days in the vineyards. At Guiliano Coppini's country estate near Florence, workers toast the new vintage during the traditional repast served on the last day of the wine harvest.*

EXTERIORS

ABOVE: *Like many villas in Portofino, this mountainside house is surrounded by trees and shrubs that offer beauty and privacy.* **LEFT:** *Painted stucco palazzi line the quay in Portofino. Many restaurants and shops are located on the ground floor of these centuries-old structures.* **PRECEDING PAGES:** *A classic villa on the shores of Lake Como.*

ABOVE: *The villa owned by Giselle Podbielski was one of the first built along the Costa Smeralda. Old Sardinian tiles cover the roof.*
RIGHT: *The patio of the villa has recessed areas in the stucco walls.*

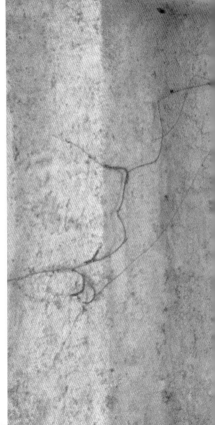

Villa Belvedere has been home to author Alessandro Manzoni, composer Vincenzo Bellini, and the younger sons of England's King George IV. Built in the late 1700s and enlarged during the following century, the villa is presently owned by Jean-Marc Droulers, the chairman of the Villa d'Este Corporation.

This compact farmhouse, dating from the 1600s, was purchased by a young Milanese couple, Luca and Renee Mattioli. It had been uninhabited for 30 years when the Mattiolis bought it, and it needed a complete restoration—accomplished, according to Renee Mattioli, on a very limited budget.

ABOVE: *The Umbrian farm of François and Shirley Caracciolo includes the Church of St. Blaze, which dates from 1050.* **RIGHT:** *Villa Balbiano is one of Lake Como's few remaining Renaissance villas. The building's symmetrical design allows glimpses of the lake from the front lawn.*

La Cassinella, the Lake Como villa of Giacomo Mantegazza, was built in the 19th century. The rich salmon stucco exterior is trimmed in ivy and brightened with blue shutters. Stately cypresses are found throughout the property.

ABOVE: *The Sardinian house designed by Savin Couëlle, one of the island's best-known architects, was built into the coastline's existing rock formation.* **RIGHT:** *A large waterside villa in Conca dei Marini, owned by a French family, was once a rope factory. The villa's windows and terraces overlook the Gulf of Salerno.*

Sardinian villas are typically constructed from local stone and designed to harmonize with the landscape. Walls are often curved around pre-existing rock formations.

In the Sardinian villa of Giselle Podbielski, a patio overlooks the Liscia di Vacca bay. The outdoor dining table is used frequently by the family, which has entertained a number of well-known guests such as Greta Garbo and Catherine Deneuve; visitors come for informal lunches and afternoon swims in the bay.

CLOCKWISE FROM TOP LEFT: *An entrance to a Renaissance villa on Lake Como; a shuttered façade in Portofino; an entrance to an Umbrian palazzo.* **FAR LEFT:** *In the Chianti countryside, a stone defense tower, part of which dates from A.D. 970, belongs to Raymond Flower, an English author.*

A granary in the countryside near Florence is now used as a guest house by the Del Bono family, who restored this structure as well as the casa colonica (not shown) adjacent to it. The photograph above shows the granary before the restoration.

The stone villa built by the late Count Tondani in the 1930s is considered one of the most beautiful in Courmayeur. Religious frescoes, decorative stone balconies, and intricately carved doors enrich the façade.

ABOVE: *The cloisters of the Villa Tondani in Courmayeur.* **LEFT:** *A snow-topped terrace on a house in Courmayeur.*

GARDENS

ABOVE: *A grape arbor in the garden of the Prinetti home in Badia a Coltibuono is a reminder of the property's early days as a vineyard.* **RIGHT:** *A passageway leads to the bedrooms of a villa near the Porto Cervo harbor.* **PRECEDING PAGES:** *A Lake Como villa has a garden with a good deal of lawn, atypical of the region, which is characterized by more formal gardens.*

ABOVE: *In the hills above Portofino, a garden in bloom.* **LEFT:** *Now the home of the Prinetti family, a major producer of Chianti Classico, a former abbey in the heart of the Chianti is flanked by formal gardens. Historical sources show that the first vineyards in the upper Chianti were planted here.*

71

Clockwise from top left: *In a villa along the Amalfi coast, a wrought-iron grille and ivy vines frame a dining room window; a stone mask accents the wall of a villa on Lake Como; in a waterside garden on Lake Como, a beach chair is ready for use.* **Far left:** *An antique carriage and terra-cotta urn stand in a corner of an old stable.*

The tall shuttered doors of a farmhouse in Umbria, owned by François and Shirley Caracciolo, open to a vine-covered terrace. The house was restored with materials from old buildings found in the region.

ABOVE: *Terra-cotta urns planted with geraniums are common in lakeside gardens.*
RIGHT: *Narrow steps are a typical element in Amalfi.*
FAR RIGHT: *A rich variety of flowers and trees flourish in a garden in Positano.*

The Tuscan casa colonica *owned by Paolo and Fioretta Panerai is surrounded by a garden where clusters of rosemary, lavender, jasmine, oleander, and iris grow among the rocks.*

ABOVE: *A trellis covered with roses in a Lake Como garden.* **RIGHT:** *Lily ponds with stone fountains are found in the gardens of many lakeside villas.*

Clockwise from top left: *A cluster of rich green lily pads float on a garden pool; stone putti, or cherubs, decorate many lily ponds; this putto is made of Vicenza stone.* **Far left:** *The entranceway to a villa in Positano has a cooling fountain.*

ABOVE: *Doric columns line a loggia at the back of the Mantegazza villa on Lake Como.* **LEFT:** *The elaborate formal gardens of the Borromeo Palace on an island in Lake Maggiore.*

Above: *A small terrace on the Amalfi coast overlooks the Gulf of Salerno. It contains plants and trees that will later be rooted in the villa's garden and is a favorite spot for breakfasts and lunches.* **Right:** *The arched passageway of one of the first villas on the Costa Smeralda was painted with a wash of terra-cotta, yellow, and ochre paint.*

ABOVE: *A Positano terrace has the same blue tiles that were used for the interior's flooring. A contemporary wrought-iron rocking chair contrasts with the antique capital found in the area.*

LEFT: *The shaded patio of the Sardinian villa owned by architect Luigi Vietti has a view of the entrance to the Porto Cervo harbor.*

LOOKING
INSIDE

THE interior of an Italian country house can range from the rustic simplicity of a Tuscan casa colonica to an antiques-filled lakeside villa. Tuscan or Umbrian farmhouses are often furnished with rough-hewn furniture, handmade wooden decorative objects, and colorful majolica plates and pottery. Stone walls, beamed ceilings, and terracotta tiled floors are found even in the living and dining areas, and eat-in kitchens are a relatively new use for a room viewed as a service unit for centuries.

Mountain house decor, at its most fanciful, is sometimes referred to as lo stile della nonna, grandmother's style, because of its assortment of tufted furniture, lacy antimacassars, hand-painted cupboards, ceramic stoves, and romantic bedrooms. Beds with hand-carved headboards are draped in covers made from antique fabrics and embroidered cottons. Hand-painted wardrobes crafted in the South Tyrol and Alto Adige are decorated with natural and religious motifs. A traditional, and still essential, element of both mountain living rooms and bedrooms is the stufa, or stove, often covered in beautiful ceramic tile.

A house in Portofino or Positano may have fine antiques, paintings, and rugs, or may be styled more casually with white canvas sofas and chairs, locally handcrafted rugs, pillows, and bedcoverings, brightly tiled floors, and rough stucco walls. This comfortable Mediterranean look is particularly popular in Sardinia. The lake region offers a white-glove approach to Italian country living. Although life on the lake is far more relaxed than it was a hundred years ago, many houses are still furnished with period antiques and surrounded by formal gardens.

Regardless of the region, Italian country interior style defies easy replication with the purchase of a certain sofa or type of fabric. It does invite an imaginative and idiosyncratic approach to mixing a variety of country elements.

PRECEDING PAGES: *A study in a Sardinian villa has walls decorated with models of Genoan ships and floors covered with locally crafted rugs.*

LIVING

RIGHT: *The walls and ceilings of the dining and living area of the Sardinian villa designed by Savin Couëlle are made of cement and plaster. As he does for all his architectural designs, Couëlle sought "a marriage of structure with terrain."* **PRECEDING PAGES:** *The living room of an Umbrian villa near Todi was once a granary. Building materials from the 15th and 16th centuries were used in the restoration.*

ABOVE: *A decorative banister in the entranceway of a Lake Como villa dates from the 1920s.* **RIGHT:** *To add interest to the white stucco walls of a villa along the Amalfi coast, architect Julio la Fuente embedded stone from the region in the arched passageway leading to the terrace.*

The second-floor hall of a Lake Como villa, with doors opening to lake views, has a classical flavor. The console and mirror date from the early 1800s. The marble floors are not only decorative but good insulators as well, according to the owner, Michele Canepa, who says the second level stays quite warm throughout the winter without heat from radiators.

Clockwise from top left: *A master bedroom in a Lake Como villa; chairs from the 1700s in a Lake Como salon. Venini vases made from Murano glass on an 18th-century mantel. The walls are covered with neoclassical frescoes.*
Far right: *Hand-carved doors provide a contrast to white stucco walls.*

These Egyptian artifacts in the second-floor study of a medieval Tuscan tower are the oldest objects in a very old house.

The commode, lacquered in red and adorned with elaborate scenes, was crafted in Venice in the 18th century. In the Veneto, country furniture is frequently decorated with lively motifs and rich colors. Often religious or allegorical, the designs and appliqués have a naive quality.

ABOVE: *A 17th-century hand-painted coffered ceiling was installed in a contemporary apartment in Cortina d'Ampezzo to give it an antique flavor.* **RIGHT:** *In the same apartment, walls were covered with 18th-century paneling.*

The stone walls of a Tuscan farmhouse were painted with pink-, sepia-, and terra-cotta–toned earth dyes. The 18th-century hand-painted commode is Venetian.

The passageway outside the living room of a Sardinian villa was painted a light ochre and is lined with rustic Italian antiques.

ABOVE: *The fireplace in a Tuscan farmhouse dates from the 13th century. An antique copper pot, originally used to heat water and cook polenta, still hangs beneath the wood mantelpiece.*
LEFT: *An antique Tuscan madia, or bread bin, now serves as a little desk in a farmhouse entrance hall.*

ABOVE: *A large 18th-century chandelier illuminates the second-level main salon of a villa on Lake Como.* **LEFT:** *In a Positano villa, hats from around the world are displayed in a small room.*

Stucco walls and terra-cotta tile flooring are typical elements in a Tuscan farmhouse. A bounty of wild yellow marguerites adds color to the entrance hall of this villa in the heart of Chianti country.

ABOVE: Cotto, *the rough-hewn red bricks frequently used as flooring in Tuscan farmhouses, is left unadorned. A Tuscan kitchen cupboard now stores china.* **LEFT:** *Numerous umbrellas and golf clubs fill an antique rustic barrel in the entrance hall of a Lake Como villa.*

121

ABOVE: *In a Lake Como villa, the entrance hall contains a 16th-century Tuscan library table.* **LEFT:** *Originally a veranda, the second-floor study in a farmhouse 20 minutes from Florence has thick stone walls covered with plaster. The thick walls keep the house cool during the summer months.*

The large terrace of a villa in Conca dei Marini has bamboo furniture covered with canvas cushions and pillows that were embroidered in the region. The terrace is cooled and protected by a bamboo roof, not shown.

ABOVE: *In an Umbrian villa, a former animal stall is now the living room and is filled with Italian, French, and English antiques. The sofa is covered with French fabric.* **RIGHT:** *An early 19th-century sofa is one of the few pieces of furniture in the ground-floor salon of a Renaissance villa on Lake Como.* **OVERLEAF, LEFT:** *Brightly patterned tiles made in the Amalfi region add an informal touch to the 18th-century antiques-filled living room of a Positano villa.* **OVERLEAF, RIGHT:** *Formal touches in country settings.*

DINING

RIGHT: *A small eat-in kitchen in an apartment in Cortina d'Ampezzo has contemporary paneling.* **PRECEDING PAGES:** *Rustic 18th-century pieces are used in the main dining room of a Tuscan farmhouse.*

LEFT: *Four decades' worth of Chianti Classico vintages are stored in a Badia a Coltibuono cantina.* **BELOW:** *The Del Bono family enjoys an outdoor meal at their Tuscan farmhouse.* **FAR LEFT:** *A simple kitchen in the Valle d'Aosta.*

In a Cortina d'Ampezzo chalet, a former hayloft was converted into a dining area. The table was made from an antique wood plank that was 3½ meters (10½ feet) long.

ABOVE: *White lacquer paneling covers cabinets and walls in the small kitchen of Gianfranco Ferrè's house on Lake Maggiore.*
RIGHT: *Wood and copper kitchen utensils made in the Valle d'Aosta decorate the walls of a Courmayeur kitchen.*

This stone window with its wrought-iron grille was found in a Valdostano castle and installed in the wall between the living and dining rooms of an area chalet. The owners of the villa, year-round residents, collect antique artifacts and pottery from the region.

A hearty antipasto prepared by the Maison de Filippo restaurant at the foot of Mont Blanc includes tomini with herbs, pepperoni, and zucchini flavored with bagna cauda, prosciutto crudo, *assorted salamis, rice and bean salads, and* prosciutto cotto *served with boiled potatoes and cauliflower. For many, a sampling of these appetizers suffices as a full meal.*

Above: *Giselle Podbielski and family friends enjoy a casual lunch in an outdoor dining area of her villa on the Costa Smeralda.*
Right: *The patio of Gianfranco Ferrè's villa on Lake Maggiore is large enough for only a small luncheon table, but it affords a panoramic view of the lake.*

Although kitchens are still regarded as service rooms in many parts of the Italian countryside, those in newer houses along the Costa Smeralda are large enough to eat in; they are equipped with modern appliances and are usually filled with colorful tiles.

The Carrara marble sink dates from the time the Badia a Coltibuono villa, now owned by the Prinetti family, was an abbey. The villa passed into private hands in the early 1800s.

The tiles in the kitchen of this Costa Smeralda villa, designed and built by Luigi Vietti, one of Sardinia's pioneering and most prominent architects, were made locally but have a Neapolitan motif.

ABOVE: *A bunch of onions hang from a beam in the kitchen of a farmhouse near Todi.* **LEFT:** *The hand-carved 17th-century Valdostano chest is topped with a collection of pewter plates and pitchers crafted in the Valle d'Aosta in the 17th, 18th, and 19th centuries.*

153

During the spring and summer, a small pergola overlooking a garden and Lake Como serves as an outdoor dining room for an early Renaissance palazzo.

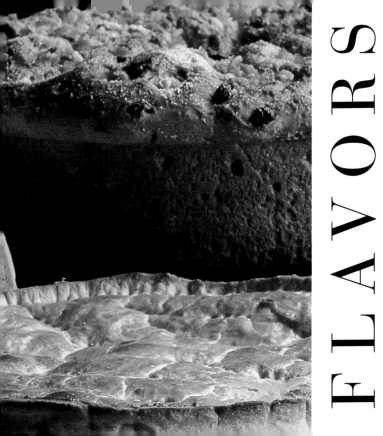

FLAVORS

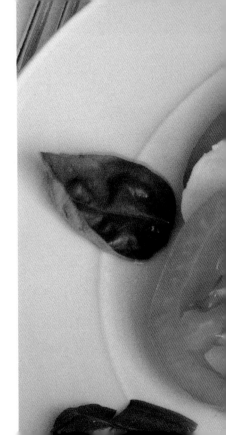

RIGHT: *A classic spring and summer favorite in lake country: fresh mozzarella, basil, and tomatoes. It is served as an appetizer or entrée.* **PRECEDING PAGES:** *Tasty breads and pies are a specialty along the Amalfi coast. The pizza rustica, foreground, has a sugar crust and is a delectable mixture of prosciutto, red pepper, cheese, and raisins.*

ABOVE: *An impromptu drying room was established behind one of the arches of a Tuscan farmhouse loggia. Freshly picked tomatoes, pears, and apples from the farmhouse's garden fill the table.* **LEFT:** *Preserves made from fresh tomatoes at the end of the summer are stored in* acqua minerale *bottles.*

ABOVE: *A* minestra di pane *simmers on a Tuscan cook's stove.* **LEFT:** *For* fagioli all'uccelletto, *the beans (*fagioli*) are cooked with sage, an herb also used to season* uccelli *(larks) during the hunting season. This is probably why the popular Tuscan and Umbrian bean dish, eaten year-round, was given its misleading name.*

Along the Italian Mediterranean coast in summer, pasta is often seasoned with fresh vegetables. Spaghetti with artichokes and asparagus is a favorite dish in Positano restaurants.

Scampi a cartoccio, *a mixture of langoustines (prawns), basil, and linguini, is served at Positano's San Pietro Hotel.*

A platter of fresh prosciutto crudo (ham that has been salted and air-dried) and thin slices of soprassata sausage is served as a light appetizer at the Badia a Coltibuono restaurant in Gaiole in Chianti.

This appetizer, made with thick Tuscan bread, olive oil, and tomatoes, is eaten in late summer and fall. It is called fettunta *in Tuscany and* bruschetta *in Umbria.*

CLOCKWISE FROM TOP LEFT: *Crunchy* biscotti *are often eaten with* vin santo, *a sweet wine; bread is an important element in meals; in the mountains, a coffee and* grappa *mixture is drunk communally from a* grolla, *a hand-carved wooden cup typical of the Valle d'Aosta.* **FAR LEFT:** *Polenta is a staple in Alpine regions.*

171

Fontina is used in a wide variety of dishes in the Valle d'Aosta. Zuppa valdostano, a hearty soup in which fontina is a main ingredient, also contains cauliflower and toasted whole-wheat bread, and is topped with nutmeg.

SLEEPING

Above: *Walls of the master bathroom of a Cortina d'Ampezzo chalet are covered with old logs.* **Right:** *The same bedroom has a baldachin of white Lombardy lace and cotton piqué.* **Preceding pages:** *The master bedroom of a Lake Como villa is furnished with antiques from northern and central Italy.*

In his bedroom, Giacomo Mantegazza has chosen simple lines and subtle colors that contrast graciously with the elaborately carved mantel.

In a Renaissance palazzo on Lake Como, an elaborate 18th-century Spanish bed is covered with a handmade Lombardy lace bedcover and cushions. Spanish antiques are often found in Lombardy's lakeside villas; the region was once occupied by Spain.

In a bedroom in a Cortina d'Ampezzo chalet, the bed linens and hand-embroidered piqué pillowcases are Venetian, with the exception of the big cushion, which was handmade in the Marches.

ABOVE: *A Genoan four-poster in the guest bedroom of a chalet overlooking Cortina is typical of Italian beds made during the 16th and 17th centuries.* **LEFT:** *A Venetian lace antimacassar serves as a runner on a bedroom chest. The silver hand mirror is also Venetian.*

A small guest room in a Cortina d'Ampezzo chalet can sleep two. The little table was made from an old hatbox, and the chair is a mid-18th-century regional piece.

ABOVE: *In the Villa Belvedere's guest bedroom, a 19th-century Spanish bed purchased in Madrid is covered with locally crafted lace.* **RIGHT:** *The bedroom's chair and its fabric, framed by white cotton curtains, date from the Queen Anne period.*

An Italian lace and linen bedspread and pillows cover the neo-Gothic wrought-iron baldachin bed in a bedroom in a Portofino villa.

191

ARTS & CRAFTS

Whether glazed in a single color, intricately patterned, or in rich terra-cotta earth tones, ceramic tiles are an important element in Italian homes.
PRECEDING PAGES: *Venetian decorative pavement is a source of design ideas for many artisans and tile manufacturers.*

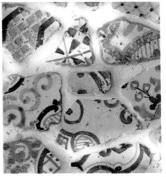

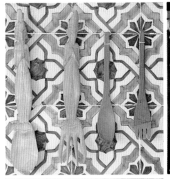

CLOCKWISE FROM TOP LEFT: *Colorful
Sardinian tiles; a decorative
stufa, or stove, like those found
in most Ampezzano homes—
this one was made in Genoa in
the 1500s; a detail of a blue-
and-white ceramic bench for
which artisans re-created an
early 18th-century design.*

A handsome ceramic wash-basin, hand-painted with the coat of arms of the Count Frigeri di Gattatico, was made near Amalfi.

ABOVE: *Colorfully painted majolica, decorated with floral motifs or religious and mythic ones, has been produced in the Tuscan and Umbrian countryside for centuries. Today there are many small factories and shops devoted exclusively to the production and sale of pottery.*

CLOCKWISE FROM TOP LEFT: *A dish ideal for serving soup or pasta is trimmed in a classic Tuscan blue-and-white scroll pattern; a lively flowers-and-fruit motif covers a glazed pitcher destined to serve liters of Chianti; an artisan reproduces an antique design on an urn covered with white glaze.*

Local artisans throughout Italy created a taste for elaborate wrought-iron treatments. **CLOCKWISE FROM TOP LEFT:** *Details of a wrought-iron fence and gate, and a Louis XV–style garden chair.* **FAR RIGHT:** *A wrought-iron grille covers a glassless window in a Savin Couëlle villa in Sardinia.*

Examples of arte povera, *an imitation of the japanning and Eastern lacquering techniques that were much in vogue in Venice and its surrounding regions in the 1700s.* Arte povera *embellishment made Venetian and Veneto commodes, wardrobes, and storage chests among the most decorative you'll see in Italy.*

ABOVE: *An antique typographer's storage box displays a collection of porcelain figurines and marionette heads.*
RIGHT: *A Tuscan crèche demonstrates the 18th-century taste for dressing figurines in richly detailed clothing.*

204

LEFT: *A small desk from a farmer's house is topped with a locally crafted doll and storage box.* **BELOW:** *Mountain wildflowers, dried and arranged in small bouquets, are frequently found in Italian alpine houses.*

CLOCKWISE FROM TOP LEFT: *Embroidered linens for sale in Portofino; a Sardinian fabric with the popular raised* pibiònes *effect, so named because it resembles clusters of grapes; checking the pattern of an unfinished sweater in Umbria.* **FAR RIGHT:** *Italian pewter and majolica trim the shelf of a Tuscan* armadio.